OCCASIONAL PAPER 2
written by Ian Smith

Changing our minds about intelligence

Cover design: Eva Ming Ling Kam
Book layout design: Susana Siew-Demunck

Originally published by Learning Unlimited
Republished in Australia by

HAWKER BROWNLOW
•
E D U C A T I O N

P.O. Box 580, Cheltenham,
Victoria 3192, Australia
Phone: (03) 9555 1344 Fax: (03) 9553 4538
Toll Free Ph: 1800 33 4603 Fax: 1800 15 0445
Website: http://www.hbe.com.au
Email: brown@hbe.com.au

© 2002 Learning Unlimited
© 2003 Hawker Brownlow Education

Printed in Australia
All right reserved

Code: #LUA-8878

National Library of Australia Cataloguing-in-Publication data:

Smith, Ian, 1947 Sep. 14–.
Changing our minds about intelligence.

For primary and secondary school teachers.
ISBN 1 74025 887 8.

1. Intellect. 2. Child development. I. Title. (Series:
Smith, Ian, 1947 Sep. 14– Occasional paper; 2).

370.152

Contents

Foreword

This is the first in a series of occasional papers being published by Learning Unlimited and Hawker Brownlow Education. These papers are being produced in response to a growing demand from teachers to be brought up to date with our current understandings about how children learn and how good teachers teach.

It has been pointed out that you would not go to a doctor who had failed to keep up to date with what we know about medicine over the past twenty years. Yet a large percentage of the teachers in Scotland have been in post for more than twenty years, and many have not had the opportunity to update their knowledge about learning and teaching in that time.

There will be two kinds of occasional papers. Some will focus on what we know. They will draw on a wide body of research to summarise our current understandings about a key aspect of learning and teaching. Written on the assumption that most teachers do not have the time or the energy to read lengthy academic texts at the end of a busy day, they will be short and, we hope, readable. Further references will be given for those who feel inclined to explore further.

It is clear, however, that teachers not only need help to reflect on the ideas that underpin what they do in the classroom, they need practical help and support to put them into practice in the classroom. For this reason some of the papers will focus on ideas and techniques, which work in the classroom, and some will describe case studies of good practice in schools.

Given the name of our company, it was important for us to tackle, very early on in this series, the issue of what it means to be clever in our society. Our beliefs about cleverness are very deep-seated. On a number of occasions over the past few years, when talking with teachers in Scotland, about the huge potential of the human brain, I have been asked the same question: 'surely you are not saying that everyone can become a brain surgeon?'. The fact that I have been asked the question so often illustrates the way we think about intelligence. Yes there are limits to what individuals can learn, but none of us will ever know what these limits are, let alone reach them. In that sense, learning is unlimited.

I am grateful to Robin Lloyd Jones and Bob Bissell for their support and help in putting this paper together; to Liz Callaghan for proof reading, and to Joan Black, Centre for Education and Training Development, Glasgow Caledonian University for desk-top publishing and publication.

We are happy to consider suggestions for future titles in the series from potential authors, whether classroom practitioners or academics.

Ian Smith, January 2001

Why we need to change our minds about intelligence

'We sorely need a new view of intelligence in our schools, our universities and our businesses. A view of intelligence that is less exclusive, far more democratic, and with far wider application to the real world.'

Robert Sternberg

This paper will argue that it is important for us to change our minds about intelligence for the following reasons:

❑ Intelligence is of great practical importance to us all in our everyday lives. We see lots of examples of unintelligent behaviour around us. If we are honest, all of us could do with a bit more intelligence.

❑ Our beliefs about intelligence (what it is, and how we come to be intelligent) run deep and they have a profound effect on the way we see ourselves, the way we relate to other people, on our beliefs about society in general and how our country should be run. Intelligence is by no means simply an educational issue: it is a political one too.

❑ Our views about intelligence also have cultural origins. What counts for intelligence in Western society is very different from what counted as intelligence in previous centuries or what counts as intelligence in other parts of the world today.

❑ The traditional view of intelligence this century in our society has been narrow and simplistic, limiting and pessimistic. It can lead young people to believe that working hard and making an effort doesn't count and it can lead parents and teachers to believe that they can't make much of a difference.

❑ Our education system, despite the many changes it has gone through and despite the rhetoric of politicians and school mission statements, still perpetuates the traditional view: a view which stands in the way of raising achievement for all in our schools.

❑ This traditional view is outdated. We need a different view: less simplistic and less narrow, less limiting and more optimistic and based on empirical evidence. However, this doesn't mean throwing out the old view entirely.

The paper will address the questions below. It will look at the traditional view in some depth and the myths on which it is based. It will examine some of the new evidence and new ideas which make up what has been called the 'emerging science of learnable intelligence' and will encourage you to open your mind and reflect on these ideas in the light of your own beliefs. Finally it will look at some ways in which we can encourage teachers and pupils to reflect on this crucial topic.

❑   What is our traditional view of intelligence, ability and achievement?

❑   How has this view affected the achievement of young people in school?

❑   How does our view of intelligence relate to what we actually know about it?

❑   Can changing our minds about intelligence help schools to raise achievement?

❑   If so, how do we change our minds?

#LUA-8878 © 2003 Hawker Browlow Education

The traditional view of intelligence

intelligence: intellect, understanding, quickness of mind
ability: sufficient capacity to do something; competence

Shorter Oxford English Dictionary

Often, when trying to define what a word means, dictionaries are useful starting points, but no more than that. They describe the meaning of words rather than the things for which the words have come to stand. The word *intelligence* is one that has come to mean many things in our society over the past hundred years. Behind that one word lie a range of powerful and deep-seated beliefs, implicit theories, mental models or assumptions about the world, about our education system, about how we learn, even about our worth as individuals.

We all think we know what intelligence and ability is in everyday language. If we describe someone as intelligent, able, smart, bright, clever, sharp, brainy or someone else as unintelligent, lacking in ability, thick, stupid, dull, obtuse, slow then everyone knows what we mean. We tend to be describing not only someone who has or does not have 'brain power' but someone who has a particular kind of 'brain power' – the kind of knowledge and understanding of words and logic that helps you to do well in school and in the academic world.

Our beliefs about intelligence are based on a series of myths and give us a distorted and inaccurate view of the world, of how people learn and most seriously of our own potential and capabilities. None of us is born with these beliefs. We learn them as we go through life. But for many of us they are deep seated and hard to un-learn. More than any other set of beliefs they limit what we can learn, what we can do and what we can achieve, so it's worth examining the myths that underlie these beliefs in some detail. In this section we explore the two most powerful myths of all, that intelligence is fixed and that intelligence is general.

Intelligence is fixed

Most people believe that intelligence is fixed at birth or soon afterwards and that it is not learnable, that we have to put up with what we have got or make the best of it.

Psychologists have described this way of thinking about intelligence as 'entity theory' and contrast it with what they call 'incremental theory':

entity theory: intelligence is a fixed entity or uncontrollable characteristic, a thing that never changes
incremental theory: intelligence is a malleable, improvable and controllable characteristic

The 'ability counts most' model of achievement (entity model)	The 'effort makes a big difference' model of achievement (incremental model)
understanding is something that just happens	understanding usually comes gradually, a bit at a time
if you are smart you get it, if you are not you don't	you can understand a little or a lot, you can never understand anything completely
if you don't catch on quick, you might as well give up for the present at any rate	some people take longer to learn than others – even quick learners don't always catch on right away
effort won't get you far, ability is what really counts	to understand you often have to hang in there and persist
if you are not bright enough, there's not much anyone can do to help you	success in learning depends on effort as much as ability
if you can't do something, then it's because you're not up to it	if you can't do something it's because you're not trying hard enough or you're not getting the right kind of help

Adapted from David Perkins, *Smart Schools*

Some psychologists suggest that we are all born with an incremental theory of intelligence. Babies and infants have a huge belief in their ability to learn and are extremely good at it. In fact researchers have identified that most children bring that incremental view to school with them. But while at school many children change their theory to an entity one. Research suggests that by the age of eight many children come to believe that if they need to try hard in order to succeed, they lack ability.

I have used David Perkins' descriptions of entity and incremental theories to stimulate discussion with thousands of teachers working at all levels in the education system. It has led to profound and moving discussions where teachers have shared their own personal theories about intelligence and those of their pupils. One of the outcomes of these discussions is that teachers believe that many pupils are forming entity theories about their own intelligence even earlier than the researchers suggest and it is becoming more and more difficult for teachers in the current climate both within and outside school to shift them. When society in general has a view that intelligence is fixed it is inevitable that many parents view their children's ablity in the same way and communicate that view to them.

#LUA-8878 © 2003 Hawker Browlow Education

Intelligence is general

The second most powerful myth about intelligence is that it is automatically generalisable, that it can be applied at least by bright children to anything – for example across subjects in school and from school to the world outside school.

The idea that intelligence is general became current in the latter half of the nineteenth century when there was an attempt to apply scientific principles to human psychology. Previously, as far back as Plato and Aristotle, it had been recognised that there were differences between intellectual, emotional and moral abilities.

The idea that intelligence is both fixed and general owes most to the work of Alfred Binet and those who followed him on intelligence testing. This was for years considered by many to be psychology's greatest achievement and has been hugely influential in our education system.

Ironically, the work of Binet grew out of a desire to help and protect children, not to penalise them. He developed the original intelligence test with a view to aiding teachers to detect children in need of help.

Binet himself did not think that intelligence was either fixed or general. He had warned against the danger of such tests being used to label children as being unable to learn, recognising that giving intelligence a numerical value would lead people to think this way. He feared it would give educators the excuse to ignore the plight of poorly performing students on the grounds that they lacked the intelligence to do better. It might also give educators grounds for dismissing under-motivation and behaviour problems as symptoms of low intelligence.

As it turned out Binet was right about these risks. Indeed many would concur with Ken Richardson's view (overleaf) that IQ testing should be banned.

Why IQ tests should be banned

1 **They make very strong and often dangerous claims:**

❑ that they measure innate natural ability

❑ that they can measure it scientifically and put a number on it

❑ that they not only measure current ability but future potential.

2 **They are based on hunches not on science:**

❑ they do not take account of any theory or definition of intelligence

❑ they fail to clarify what they are measuring

❑ they assume that those who do well at school must be intelligent, and devise questions that children can answer who do well at school

❑ they then become a self-fulfilling methodology because children who do well in the tests tend to do well at school

❑ they add little to what teachers can already tell us about children in school

❑ they tell us virtually nothing about complex cognitions in the outside world.

3 **The question of IQ testing is not a harmless abstract matter but has had profound political, social and educational consequences:**

❑ IQ tests have been used to justify racism. People have been denied immigration to countries, been sterilised, had their educational, social and employment opportunities blocked, and have been denied marriage all on the basis of IQ scores.

❑ Because of intelligence testing, schooling has come to be seen by almost everyone as the ultimate test of intelligence, when in fact success in school bears very little relationship to success in any other walk of life.

❑ Tests have led teachers to look for signs of innate intelligence and to label pupils as bright or stupid.

❑ They have led to what the author of the first test, Alfred Binet, called 'brutal pessimism'.

❑ They have led parents to have low aspirations for their children (itself socially inherited and reinforced by IQ theory).

❑ A large percentage of our young people have come to believe that they are not capable of learning anything very serious or complicated.

adapted from *The Making of Intelligence* by Ken Richardson

#LUA-8878 © 2003 Hawker Browlow Education

What effects has the traditional view had on our education system?

The widely held view that intelligence is fixed, general and primarily academic is to a large extent a twentieth century phenomenon, brought about and perpetuated by our education system. It is ironic that, now we are genuinely trying to widen access to this system and to raise levels of achievement within it, the negative effects of such a view are being most keenly felt.

A wide range of evidence suggests that the traditional view has profound effects on pupil motivation and teacher expectations, on relationships between teachers and their pupils, on the assessment system, on the way we manage and organise schools and classrooms, indeed on what we value and what we want from our education system.

Pupil motivation

'A person's motivation depends on his or her intuitive beliefs about intelligence and ability.'

Stevenson and Palmer

If intelligence is fixed it follows that putting in an effort to learn is not worthwhile, and indeed if you do have to make an effort you can't be intelligent.

Research indicates the significant effect that entity view of intelligence can have on the self-confidence and motivation of pupils of all abilities:

'Children who appear indifferent to learning and who are labelled as lazy or unmotivated by their teachers, may in fact be protecting themselves against feelings of failure as a result of self-attributions of poor ability. Even very able students may give up as a result of such ability attributions.'

Stevenson and Palmer

Detailed research linking pupils' theories about intelligence with their attitudes to problem-solving and their ability to problem-solve point to stark differences:

A small but in-depth study of the early years in secondary school, described in *Effective Teaching and Learning* (Cooper and McIntyre 1996), suggests that the conditions within which teachers work force them into a generalised typing of pupils in terms of these beliefs about ability, often based on very inadequate information. Once pupils have been typed, teachers are very reluctant to change their views about them, and adjust their expectations of pupils accordingly.

Children who hold entity theory	Children who hold incremental theory
adopt 'performance' goals, because they believe that all they can do is demonstrate how much ability they have	adopt 'learning' goals, because they believe that they can improve their ability by their own efforts
focus on being right; feel clever when they get the correct answer and do better than their peers	focus on understanding; feel clever when they have worked hard and mastered something for themselves
report failure as down to their own inadequacy	view challenging tasks as an opportunity for improvement
become bored with problems	work out strategies to solve problems and keep themselves motivated
feel helpless; worry about their own performance	feel optimistic and self-confident; view unsolved problems as challenges
avoid the task and become less able to solve problems	focus on the task and became more able to solve problems

Teacher expectations

'Too often we become what other people expect. And when those expectations are telegraphed clearly by parents and teachers through word, attitude, atmosphere and body language, then the expectations become the student's limitations.'

Gordon Dryden and Jeanette Voss, *The Learning Revolution*

Research over a number of years has shown that if teachers have higher expectations of pupils they will do better and vice versa. What the research is saying is that, through their expectations, teachers not only predict pupil achievement, they cause it. They are a self-fulfilling prophecy. This may not operate in all classrooms with all teachers at all times. Nevertheless there is little doubt that the 'teacher expectancy effect' can and does operate.

The curriculum

Our view that intelligence is a matter of academic ability has led to a narrow view of the curriculum. Despite valiant attempts to achieve breadth and balance in the curriculum, the academic subjects in general and those that focus on words and logic are considered to be more important. We continue to put too much emphasis on a narrow range of abilities, which excludes certain learners and fails to develop the full potential of all learners.

Our view of intelligence also explains our continuing emphasis on content rather than process. What is the point in teaching people to learn how to learn if intelligence is fixed?

Finally, our view that intelligence is not only academic but automatically transferable to different subjects and different contexts has led us to underplay the role of expertise and know-how in schools, and not to sufficiently recognise the importance of relating academic learning to everyday life outside the school.

Assessment

The idea that intelligence is fixed and general, allied to the legacy of intelligence testing, has influenced both teachers' and the public's attitude to assessment. As a result, too many people equate assessment with tests or exams and see its purpose as being to sort the 'sheep from the goats' rather than to help people improve their learning.

Ability tests were not traditionally used primarily to tell us about the talent of the person being tested but in relation to the talent of other people. The success of a test was whether it produced a perfect bell curve sorting out the small number of bright people and dull people from the mass in the middle, rather than to determine how well an individual learns. This tradition lives on in our assessment and examination systems. It also lives on in our attitudes to testing and examinations. Witness our mixed responses to the larger number of pupils passing the national examinations – it's not that we are getting smarter or the teaching is getting better, we must be 'dumbing down' the tests.

This overuse of testing for sorting rather than improvement and the focus on competition in the classroom appear to support the view that intelligence is fixed and leads to self-attributions concerning ability.

Setting and streaming

In the past, school policies on setting and streaming were based on an assumption that intelligence is fixed and general and can be measured accurately. In practice, setting and streaming encouraged labelling and reinforced limiting beliefs. Teachers lowered their expectations of the lower sets and had unrealistically high expectations of some pupils in the top sets.

Grouping pupils by ability within classes and even between classes on occasions can be a more effective way to operate. In recent years there has been renewed interest in setting. 'Achievement for All' (SOEID 1996) put a strong emphasis on attainment grouping and many schools believe that they can raise achievement for all by setting and making sure the lower sets get better quality support and attention.

When introducing such policies, however, schools need to take very careful account of how this fits in practice with the views of staff, pupils and parents about intelligence.

The culture of schooling

In the twentieth century schooling has come to be the ultimate test of intelligence. If you don't 'do well' at school you cannot be intelligent. But 'doing well' at school has come to have a particular meaning in most people's minds and the ethos in most schools reflects this.

Many schools have a stated mission to value all children and help them to achieve their full potential. But in practice, often because of outside pressures, this means doing well in a narrow range of subjects. Academic intelligence is supported and valued ahead of practical and emotional intelligence.

Many schools are taking specific steps to build an ethos of achievement, which is based on a broader view of what constitutes intelligence. They find ways to support and celebrate a range of intelligences. But there is a limit to what individual schools can do: too often they seem to be swimming against a strong current. What we need is a new culture of schooling, which is based on a new view of intelligence.

#LUA-8878 © 2003 Hawker Browlow Education

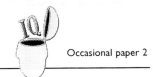

Towards a new view

The idea that intelligence might be learnable has not yet been embraced by our society widely and deeply. The traditional view is very difficult to shift. It continues to get in the way.

But work being done in such diverse areas as neurology, genetics and education is beginning to come together to provide us with a deeper understanding of human intelligence.

As a result, a growing body of academics and educators no longer subscribe to the traditional view. Some even suggest that we should no longer use the word 'intelligence': that the very word now gets in the way. Howard Gardner, a leading authority on intelligence, has in effect invented a new word – 'intelligences' (you will find that your spell checker has not yet caught up with this fact!). Her Majesty's Inspectorate in Scotland have for some time now eschewed the use of the word 'intelligence' altogether in official documents preferring the word 'abilities' instead. This reflects a growing uneasiness about what the word 'intelligence' has come to mean.

Some people have tried to replace the traditional view with an equally easy simple and accessible view – that we all have unlimited potential, we are capable of anything if we get the right kind of help and believe in ourselves enough. But such a view is as dangerously simplistic as the traditional view. It is not based on empirical evidence and can simply increase cynicism and despair.

David Perkins has suggested that what we need is a 'new science of intelligence'. It will help us address questions such as, 'What are the mechanisms that underlie intelligence?' 'Can people learn to be more intelligent?' 'What aspects of intelligence need special attention?'

But such a science is only now emerging; it is still by no means clear what the answers to these questions will be. IQ is still not a discredited concept; witness the success of *The Bell Curve* (1994) in the United States. While only a few academics still subscribe to the traditional view, there is no one simple alternative being offered by academics. Indeed as Perkins himself admits:

'Conceptions of intelligence today are in flux with new theories asserting their rights like African bees'.

In the following sections we will look briefly at some of these theories and the evidence on which they are based.

Intelligence: both fixed and learnable

'Except in the most severe instances of genetic or organic impairment, the human brain is open to modifiability at all ages and stages of development.'

Reuven Feuerstein

In Watterson's cartoon, is Calvin wrong to believe that having to make an effort means you're not smart? Should we believe entity or incremental theory? As we have seen it's easy to ignore the evidence and take one of two sides in a potentially polarised debate.

On the one hand, we have the proponents of what David Perkins calls the 'Empire of IQ', who argue in a recent best-selling book in the United States (*The Bell Curve* 1994) that intelligence is essentially innate and largely determines how well people do in life. Inequality, therefore, is natural and inevitable, even desirable. The role that schools and teachers can play is limited. The main thing that they need to do is to avoid dumbing down the curriculum so as not to hold bright children back.

On the other hand, we have a host of educators who think schools are holding children back. Human beings, they insist, have an innate desire to learn and a natural capacity to do so. We all love to learn; it is almost involuntary. In the right environment and with the right kind of help, we are capable of extraordinary feats of intellectual and creative ability. Our potential, these educators say, goes far beyond anything ever realised.

So we have two views; the first, pessimistic and the second, optimistic. Which of the two does our current knowledge and understanding about intelligence and achievement support? The single word answer is, both. This is a complex and sensitive area and polarised and simplistic arguments are not helpful. The real issue is not whether intelligence is fixed or malleable but to what extent is it fixed and malleable, and what is the relationship between the two? Even the authors of *The Bell Curve* admit that IQ is to some extent malleable, and the supporters of the opposite view do not deny that genetics set some kind of limit on the extent to which intelligence can be realised or modified in the course of a human life.

Intelligence is partly heritable and partly environmental, but it is extremely difficult to separate the two as they interact in many different ways. Every person is a product of both nature and nurture, a carrier of genes that shape him or her but also a reservoir of innumerable experiences that cultivate various attitudes, knowledge and skills. Not only that, but children are normally raised by their genetic parents, so intelligent behaviour can come from their parents both by genetics and experience. What we don't really know is where nature leaves off and nurture begins.

As Ken Richardson puts it 'Human intelligence does not exist in genes, in brains or in social environments alone, but in the complex interactions between them'.

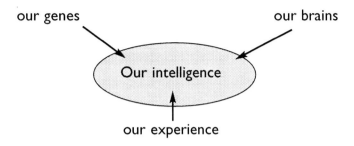

What we do know is that, although there are biological limits to every individual's capacity to learn, these limits are well above what we normally envisage. In fact there is now a huge volume of evidence from a range of sources to suggest that thinking in terms of limits is not only counterproductive, but just plain wrong.

From brain power to know-how

'Intelligence is knowing your way about: it's knowledge of experience that counts'.

David Perkins

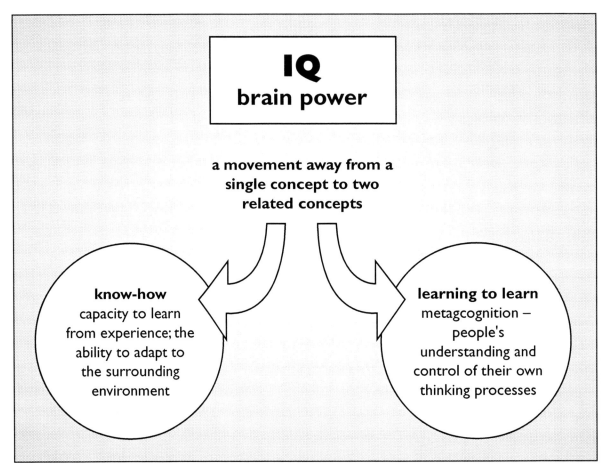

This section and the next will briefly explore the two trends shown above, which have been drawn from *Outsmarting IQ* by David Perkins.

The growth in the significance of 'know-how' or what has been called 'practical' or 'successful' intelligence stems from the fact that what is considered to be intelligence will depend very much on the circumstances – on where you are and what you are doing. What is considered to be intelligent behaviour in one context might be totally inappropriate in another. For instance, what counts as intelligence on Wall Street in New York would not count as intelligence in the Australian bush.

Robert Sternberg defines intelligence as 'purposive adaptation to and selection and shaping of real world environments relevant to one's life'. Simply stated, he is talking about people being able to apply their intelligence in the world around them in a practical way. This definition takes account not just of the context but the culture within which people find themselves and what they are actually trying to do.

What Sternberg is saying links to the decades of work that psychologists have undertaken on the notion of **expertise**. What accounts for it? Is it general intelligence, is it something more specific or is it simply knowing a lot about what you are doing? The research suggests it is

more about the latter than the former and that it is experience that counts. A good cook, a good mechanic, a good mathematician all proceed with judgement and finesse only because of a rich repertoire of experience. The dominant view in psychology used to be that good neural equipment was needed to allow you to acquire the skills and know-how in the first place. But research is now showing that the intelligent behaviour resides in the know-how rather than the neural engine.

Notions of expertise and practical intelligence have been played down within our education system where the highest form of intelligence is still considered to be academic: where know-what is more important than know-how. But more and more evidence is being gathered on the weakness of the link between success in school and success in life.

Sternberg goes out of his way to emphasise that there is nothing wrong with good test scores:

'Good test scores don't preclude successful intelligence but neither do they assure it. Indeed some people with good scores become so enamoured of those scores that they never develop the other skills they will need to be successfully intelligent'.

Both Perkins and Sternberg suggest that if we are to understand what intelligence is, we must not focus only on intelligence as a technical construct, as something that is going on inside people's heads. We must focus on behaviour – how intelligence appears visibly in the world around us. They suggest that we should ask the questions, 'What is intelligent behaviour? What does it look like?'.

In discussions with teachers about intelligence and ability I have found this an interesting and useful workshop task.

Sternberg himself did a great deal of research by asking people what were the symptoms of intelligence they would normally acknowledge. They were to answer not about what causes it or how they would measure it but what it would look like. What do people do that tells you they are intelligent? These are the main ideas that came up in his research: solve problems well, reason clearly, think logically, use good vocabulary, draw on a large store of information, balance information, are goal oriented, show intelligence in practical, not just academic ways. Sternberg suggested there will be cultural differences and you may find that you will receive some different answers.

Multiple intelligences

No single individual has done more work to challenge the idea of a single general intelligence than the Harvard professor, Howard Gardner. In *Frames of Mind* 1983 he outlined a theory of multiple intelligences. He has since described these as:

'a set of abilities, talents or mental skills each of which all normal individuals possess to some extent; individuals differ in the degree of skills and in the nature of the combination.'

Howard Gardner, *Multiple Intelligences: The Theory in Practice*

The theory is based on a study of both biological and cultural aspects of intelligence. In *Frames of Mind* he claimed to have identified seven different kinds of intelligence as follows:

Verbal/Linguistic
Thinks and learns through written and spoken words; has the ability to memorise facts, fill in workbooks, take written tests and enjoy reading. *Poets and writers.*

Logical/Mathematical
Thinks deductively; deals with numbers and recognises abstract patterns. *Mathematicians and scientists.*

Visual/Spatial
Thinks in and visualises images and pictures; has the ability to create graphic designs and communicate with diagrams and graphics. *Artists, decorators, surveyors, inventors, guides.*

Body/Kinesthetic
Learns through physical movement and body wisdom; has a sense of knowing through body memory. *Dancers, actors, sculptors, surgeons, mechanics, craftspeople.*

Musical/Rhythmic
Recognises tonal patterns and environmental sounds; learns through rhyme, rhythm and repetition. *Singers, musicians, composers.*

Interpersonal
Learns and operates one-to-one, through group relationships, and communication; also depends on all of the other intelligences. *Sales and marketing people, social workers, travel agents.*

Intrapersonal
Enjoys and learns through self-reflection, metacognition, working alone; has an awareness of inner spiritual realities. *Entrepreneurs, therapists.*

He also claimed that:

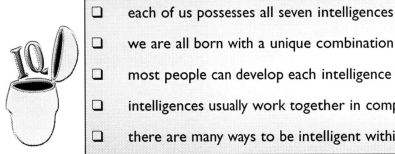

❑	each of us possesses all seven intelligences
❑	we are all born with a unique combination of the different intelligences
❑	most people can develop each intelligence to an adequate level of competency
❑	intelligences usually work together in complex ways
❑	there are many ways to be intelligent within each category.

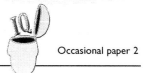

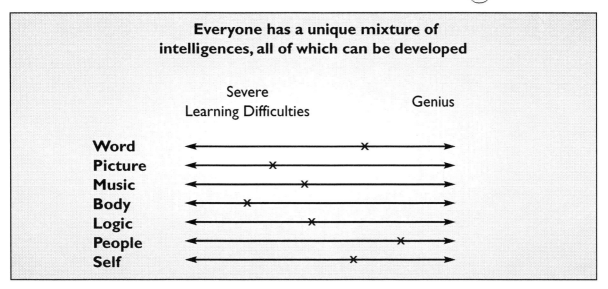

Everyone has a unique mixture of intelligences, all of which can be developed

Gardner is extremely critical of the school system based on outdated models of intelligence which see it as fixed and general. He also believes that schools put far too great an emphasis on only two intelligences – logical/mathematical and verbal/linguistic.

Despite, or maybe because of this, his theory has found widespread application in education and has been immensely influential amongst teachers in the United States. Numerous books are now published in the US on the 'seven ways of knowing' or the 'seven ways of teaching' with a chapter on each intelligence detailing practical ways in which teachers might help their pupils develop them. The theory has been less influential in Britain but there is growing interest in it here.

However, the theory is not without its critics. Other academics have pointed out that it is founded on relatively little research. Since 1994 Gardner has extended the list to eight intelligences, by claiming to have identified another kind of intelligence called 'naturalist' intelligence. He has also toyed with the idea of 'spiritual' intelligence which at one point he claimed was only a 'half intelligence'. Claims such as this do not do a great deal for the credibility of the theory.

But whether we agree with the multiple theory of intelligence or not, Gardner has done us a great service. He has broadened our ideas about intelligence and helped us to recognise the multiple nature of intelligence.

The area that remains to be explored is the balance and the relationship between the concepts of general intelligence and multiple intelligences. Gardner himself did not deny that there is such a thing as general intelligence but he does not think that general intelligence is learnable. His view is that intelligence is learnable only within intelligences.

Reflective intelligence: learning to learn

'Yes, the neural machine must be there and so must the experience, but people can learn to think and act much more intelligently. Mindware can be acquired'.

David Perkins

Both Howard Gardner and those who view intelligence as know-how, or as expertise, play down the significance of a learned general intelligence. Their view is that you do learn to be intelligent, but only in a specific context.

David Perkins believes that these views do not sufficiently value the importance of what he calls 'reflective intelligence'. He argues that it is not the case that high general intelligence and relevant knowledge in a field always lead to better reasoning. People can be very bright and very knowledgeable, but not good at handling unconventional problems in a field. Without denying the importance of specific kinds of know-how, he emphasises the importance of learning to learn.

The suggestion is that by being able to reflect on your own learning (what works and what does not work for you) you can develop a set of strategies for learning which are generic, can be applied across fields and can help you to behave generally more intelligently.

Certainly some people function metacognitively, monitoring their own thinking. They cultivate and use more strategies for tackling various intellectually demanding tasks. They benefit from positive can-do attitudes towards the best use of their own minds, recognising that thinking is often hard but emphasising the importance of persistence, systematicity and imagination. But is it something which can be taught and lead to more intelligence? Or is it the result of being highly intelligent and you just pick it up as you go along?

There are a number of well-known and respected educators throughout the world who argue strongly that reflective intelligence can be taught and claim to have proved this conclusively over the years. Two of these are Reuven Feuerstein and Edward de Bono. Both have been concerned with how people go wrong in problem-solving, providing them with tools to succeed, and showing teachers and parents the most effective use of these tools with learners.

Feuerstein has had spectacular successes over a period of forty years in Israel, working with children with learning disabilities and his program called *Instrumental Enrichment* is being increasingly used by people working in this area all over the world.

De Bono is also world renowned and works in the corporate as well as the education sector. His CoRT thinking programme has been used in schools throughout the world and was the basis of a national initiative in Venezuela. Even the writers of *The Bell Curve* admitted this initiative had probably been successful in raising the intelligence quotient of the population.

However, research on the work of Feuerstein and de Bono and the explicit teaching of metacognitive or learning strategies in general is still in its infancy. We recognise that these schemes can help people behave more intelligently, even people with severe learning difficulties, but does this amount to increasing their intelligence? Do these strategies equip people to behave more intelligently in different contexts and in the longer term? The jury is still out on these questions. Efforts to teach intelligence have been successful – but by and large not dramatically. They have improved intelligence somewhat, but have not usually changed people profoundly and for a long time.

We shall come back to the work of Feuerstein, de Bono and others in a future paper. It is no coincidence that the people arguing most for the importance of learning to learn are practising educationists. If intelligence is mainly brain power or know-how, the significance of school in raising young people's intelligence is diminished. If learning to learn is a significant factor then schools have a huge role to play.

Perkins believes that real intelligence includes brain power, know-how and learning to learn. They make up a team; they work together. He suggests that we do not know for certain how they combine forces at the moment and that more research is needed, but he also suggests that we need more attempts to teach reflective thinking systematically.

Emotional intelligence

If Perkins criticises Gardner for not putting enough emphasis on what he calls reflective intelligence, both can be criticised for underplaying the role of the emotions in learning.

In Western society there is a strong tradition of rationalism. The belief is that thinking is somehow superior to feeling which is subjective and illogical, that the emotions get in the way of thinking, and that they need to be separated from thinking and kept under control, especially the strong ones. This view is still powerfully reflected in the later stages of the education system.

Daniel Goleman can be credited with inventing and popularising the term 'emotional intelligence' with a best selling book of that title which effectively builds on Gardner's interpersonal and intrapersonal intelligences.

The book, written with an eye to the commercial sector, has had a huge impact on education in the United States. It is receiving growing attention in the UK amongst those who feel that personal and social development in schools has lost its way and is in danger of being sidelined by the back-to-basics movement and the overemphasis on academic qualifications.

Goleman defines emotional intelligence as 'Understanding one's own feelings, empathy for the feelings of others and the regulation of emotion in a way that enhances living'. (John Mayer 1990). He organises a large part of his book around the five 'domains of emotional intelligence' identified by Peter Salovey as follows:

> ❑   knowing your emotions (self-awareness)
>
> ❑   handling your emotions (self-control)
>
> ❑   recognising emotions in others (empathy)
>
> ❑   motivating oneself (learned optimism)
>
> ❑   handling relationships (social skills).

His main thesis is that emotional intelligence is critically important in all aspects of our life and that even if you focus on work alone it is a better indicator of success than academic intelligence. He believes it can be learned, but that schools do not put enough emphasis on it.

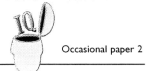

Wisdom

In our society, intelligence is not only associated with thinking but with conscious thinking; the kind of thinking that is explicit and deliberate, when you 'figure things out'. What is more, really intelligent people can figure things out quicker than others. The faster you can think the smarter you are. This belief is strengthened by the recent use of terms such as accelerated learning.

Guy Claxton in his book *Hare Brain Tortoise Mind* has pointed out that only active thinking is regarded as productive. Sitting gazing out of the classroom window or at your office wall is not considered productive. Yet many of the people we most admire, from Albert Einstein to Sherlock Holmes, practised this kind of contemplative thinking:

'We urgently want explanations, theories of everything. We find ourselves in a culture which has lost sight (not least in the education system) of fundamental distinctions, like those between being wise, being clever, having your 'wits' about you, and being merely well informed'.

Claxton suggests that the mind has three processing speeds. The first is faster than thought, the sort of unconscious reaction that happens when we walk in front of a bus. The second is what he calls deliberation, which is conscious deliberate thinking based on reason and logic. This is what we most commonly recognise as intelligence.

The third type of thinking is contemplative or meditative thinking, where we mull things over, where we may ponder a problem rather than actively try to solve it. Actually, it may involve putting the problem out of your conscious mind altogether and going for a walk or 'sleeping on it'. Claxton argues that individuals and societies in the West have lost touch with tapping into the subconscious. Only active thinking is regarded as productive.

The importance of knowing better by thinking slowly leads Claxton on to discussing the idea of wisdom. He points out that there is little empirical research on wisdom but some information on what people consider it to be. He suggests this can be summed up as follows:

> ❑ above all wisdom is practical
>
> ❑ it involves seeing through the apparent issue to the real issue underneath
>
> ❑ it is uncompromising about fundamental values but flexible and creative about the means whereby they are to be preserved or pursued
>
> ❑ it is good judgement in hard cases where important decisions have to be made on the basis of insufficient data
>
> ❑ to be wise you need to be mindful of your own world as well as that of the other person – empathy and self-awareness.

Creativity

'Imagination is more important than knowledge'.

Albert Einstein

There is a crucial connection between the contemplative thinking which Claxton describes and creativity. This is beyond the remit of this paper, but in any discussion of intelligence it is important also to look at what we mean by creativity. In our society we set great store on people being creative but, like intelligence, seem to see it as something you are either born with or you are not.

We are as confused about creativity as we are about intelligence – on the one hand seeing it as something narrow which only people such as artists, musicians and writers possess, and on the other hand as something which can apply generally to business success or family relationships: in other words you can 'lead a creative life'. There are plenty of self-help books around offering to help you become more creative on this basis.

Creative thinking is usually thought of as being deep and broad thinking while critical thinking is sound and clear thinking. David Perkins points out that neither creative nor analytical thinking stand well on their own. Good creative thinking always involves a measure of analytical thinking or else it would be misdirected; good analytical thinking always involves a measure of creative thinking or it would be too narrow.

Sternberg suggests that creative thinking not only needs to involve analytical thinking but some kind of practical thinking as well, which he defines as the ability to translate theory into practice and abstract ideas into practical accomplishments.

Certainly the growing popularity of the Einstein quote above bears testimony to the fact that many think we are in danger of underestimating the value of creative thinking in our current society at the expense of both critical and practical thinking.

One thing is certain: there is likely to be a growing debate over the coming years into what constitutes creativity and how it can be taught.

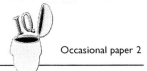

Group intelligence

The fundamental question we have been posing in this paper is 'What is intelligence?' and we have been looking at our traditional views in the light of what we know about this question at this moment in time. However, our view of intelligence is likely to undergo further change as our society continues to grow and research increases our understanding.

David Perkins has suggested that a question which will become more significant is 'Where is intelligence?'. Throughout this paper, the assumption has been that it resides inside the individual human mind. More and more writers and thinkers are challenging this assumption and making a case for what some are calling 'group' or 'distributed' intelligence. This has to do with the idea that good thinking depends as much on the others with whom we think and the artefacts and symbols that we use to think, as it does on what goes on inside our heads.

We all recognise the 'whole is greater than the sum of the parts' and many of us have practical experience of the fact that good teams have a higher intelligence than the individuals who make them up.

In his fascinating book, *Out of Control* Kevin Kelly gives us more than a glimpse of the future role of computers (which he suggests would be better called 'connectors') and artificial intelligence. He points out that the boundaries between the biological and the mechanical are already being eroded. He coins the term 'hive mind' to describe both the human brain and the internet. Biologists have known for some time that hives of bees and nests of ants have a collective intelligence well beyond the individual insects who inhabit them. He sees human intelligence expanding in the same way through the Internet and whatever replaces it in the future.

But it is time to return to the 'What?' question and focus on what we think we know at the present time.

The nub of what we know about intelligence

It is clear what intelligence is not: it is not fixed at birth or soon afterwards; it is not general and it makes little sense to view it narrowly as being about academic ability. What we do know is that intelligence is less clear-cut than we think.

❑ Individuals' abilities are much more complex, variable and changeable than is suggested in traditional notions about intelligence: what counts as intelligence will depend on the context and what you are trying to do.

❑ Intelligence is partly about brain power, but it is to a significant extent learnable. Learnable intelligence consists both of 'know-how' which can be learned and applied only in certain contexts, and of learning strategies which can be applied generally.

❑ Emotional intelligence is as important in life as what we traditionally view as academic intelligence. Making judgements and solving problems are not wholly rational activities and involve feelings as well as thinking.

❑ In Western society we need to give more credence to intuitive, slower, contemplative, subconscious thinking. It plays a great part in creativity. Wisdom is something we might seek to value more than cleverness; it involves the emotions but also contemplation.

❑ Our notions about what constitutes intelligence will keep on changing with time. In the next fifty years the question 'Where is intelligence?' will become as equally powerful as the question 'What is intelligence?'.

It is difficult to replace a traditional clear-cut view of intelligence with something less certain and more nebulous; but we must. This paper concludes by taking a brief look at the ways in which some schools are attempting to change young people's minds about intelligence.

#LUA-8878 © 2003 Hawker Browlow Education

Changing young people's minds

'I don't talk about able and less able any longer. These terms don't mean a thing. They are mince! OK, talk about more or less motivated, or more or less focused. We are all capable of being brilliant in some way'.

Secondary Headteacher

'It is understood that learners' ability is not fixed, but is alterable by the conditions of learning'.

Headline statement in Learning and Teaching
Policy at Castlebrae Community High School

We cannot change anyone's mind by exhortation, logical argument or emotional appeal alone. This is especially true where beliefs have through experience become deep-seated convictions.

Good teachers and good schools go beyond words to creating the right conditions within which young people will be prepared to re-examine their limiting beliefs and help them to experience real success, which they previously had not thought possible. They:

❏ **develop an ethos of achievement across the school** which ensures that all pupils are successful and that this success is valued. Specifically:

- the role of ability in producing success and failure is played down

- assessment plays down comparisons between pupils and highlights comparisons between present and past performance

- there is a focus on the type and amount of interaction encouraged between pupils and the quality of the relationships between teachers and pupils.

❏ **encourage and help teachers, parents and pupils to reflect together on their beliefs and assumptions about ability, motivation and potential** and how these beliefs affect the way they come across to pupils. Specifically:

- through involving everyone in open discussion about the aims and values of the school, and what 'success' means in the context of school

- by discussing and challenging our beliefs about ability at parents' meetings and with pupils in class and in personal and social development time

- by teaching pupils specific confidence-building skills in a much more systematic way across the curriculum.

❑ **think carefully before setting classes or over-using fixed ability groups** and specifically (for example:)

- avoid setting too early and take potential into account as well as attainment

- set only for one or two subjects

- where grouping by ability within classes, make sure this is not the only criterion used to make up groups

- ensure that there is movement between sets or ability groups.

❑ **create the best possible environment for classroom teachers**, where specifically:

- the number of different teacher–pupil contacts each day and each week is kept to a minimum

- teachers have enough time with pupils to assess and respond to individuals

- information about pupils is accurate, up-to-date and not limited to narrow aspects of achievement

- there are close links between the school and parents.

#LUA-8878 © 2003 Hawker Browlow Education

The discipline of hope

'I was useless at school, until I got this one teacher: she believed in me'.

Company Director

No amount of words and deeds will cut any ice with young people unless we as teachers are prepared to change our own beliefs. It is for this reason we leave the last word to one of America's best known educators, Herbert Kohl, renowned for his book *Thirty Six Children*, an account of his first year as a teacher in the Bronx in New York. His latest book called *The Discipline of Hope* is an account of his career. In it he argues that providing hope to young people is the major challenge of teaching:

'Never in my whole teaching career has it occurred to me that there are limits to what any student can do. I am hopelessly optimistic when it comes to believing in people's capacity to grow and to learn. Such optimism has occasionally led to accusations of being naïve or romantic, but I am happy to accept any accusation of being positive and hopeful in the service of my students'.

References and further reading

The Bell Curve: Intelligence and Class Structure in American Life Richard Hernstein and Charles Murray, New York, 1994

The Discipline of Hope Herbert Kohl, Simon and Schuster, 1999

Effective Teaching and Learning Paul Cooper and Donald McIntyre, Oxford University Press, 1996

Emotional Intelligence Daniel Goleman, Bloomsbury, 1996

Flying in Style Janet Aaker Smith, Hawker Brownlow Education, Melbourne, 2002

Frames of Mind Howard Gardner, Harper Collins, London, 1993

Hare Brain Tortoise Mind Guy Claxton, Fourth Estate, London, 1997

Inequality By Design: Cracking the Bell Curve Myth Claude Fischer et al, Princeton, 1996

Learning Principles, Processes and Practices Rosemary Stevenson and Joy Palmer, Cassell, 1994

Learning Styles: Personal Exploration and Practical Applications Kathleen Butler, Hawker Brownlow Education, Melbourne, 1996

The Making of Intelligence Ken Richardson, Weidenfield and Nicolson, 1999

Multiple Intelligences: The Theory in Practice Howard Gardner, Harper Collins, London, 1993

Out of Control: The New Science of Machines Kevin Kelly, Fourth Estate, London, 1994

Outsmarting IQ David Perkins, Simon and Schuster, New York, 1995

The Right to Be Intelligent Luis Alberto Machado, Pergamon, 1980

Six Thinking Hats for School Edward de Bono, Hawker Brownlow Education, Melbourne, 1992

Successful Intelligence Robert Sternberg, Simon and Schuster, New York, 1996

Teaching through the Eight Intelligences Wilma Vialle, Hawker Brownlow Education, Melbourne, 2002

Thirty Six Children Herbert Kohl, Victor Gollancz, 1968

#LUA-8878 © 2003 Hawker Browlow Education